LEGENDS OF WARFARE

AVIATION

The Blue Angels

The US Navy's Flight Demonstration Team, 1946 to the Present

KEN NEUBECK

SCHIFFER MILITARY

4880 Lower Valley Road   Atglen, PA 19310

Designed by Justin Watkinson
Type set in Impact/Minion Pro/Univers LT Std

ISBN: 978-0-7643-5658-2
Printed in China
5 4 3 2

Published by Schiffer Publishing, Ltd.
4880 Lower Valley Road
Atglen, PA 19310
Phone: (610) 593-1777; Fax: (610) 593-2002
E-mail: Info@schifferbooks.com
www.schifferbooks.com

For our complete selection of fine books on this and related subjects, please visit our website at www.schifferbooks.com. You may also write for a free catalog.

Schiffer Publishing's titles are available at special discounts for bulk purchases for sales promotions or premiums. Special editions, including personalized covers, corporate imprints, and excerpts, can be created in large quantities for special needs. For more information, contact the publisher.

We are always looking for people to write books on new and related subjects. If you have an idea for a book, please contact us at proposals@schifferbooks.com.

Acknowledgments

The Blue Angels have always been a favorite subject of mine, and I have seen them perform numerous times in the Long Island, New York, area. Over the years, I was fortunate to be able to photograph them at Republic Airport, where they were based for the Memorial Day Jones Beach Airshow. The team consisted of pilots and support personnel who always interfaced well with the public. A visit by the Blue Angels team is a major event with many moving pieces, as described in detail in this book.

The author thanks those individuals who contributed to the book, including Alan Contessa, John Gourley, Bill Larkins, Del Laughery, Mike Machat, and Josh Stoff, as well as Audrey Cohen of Epoch.5 Public Relations. The author thanks organizations such as the Cradle of Aviation Museum, the Northrop Grumman History Center, and the US Navy, as well as the latter's media websites, for their help with historical photographs. In addition, the author thanks the staff at Republic Airport in Long Island for the help that they provided to him during the Jones Beach Airshow with regard to access to the Blue Angels.

Aircraft specifications verified through *The Encyclopedia Of The World's Combat Aircraft*, Bill Gunston, 1976, Salamander Books.

Captain Greg McWherter is preparing for takeoff from Republic Airport in Long Island, NY in April of 2012. *Ken Neubeck*

Contents

Introduction

The first commander of the Blue Angels flying team was experienced Navy aviator Roy "Butch" Voris. *US Navy*

Prior to the years leading up to World War II, the US Navy at various times had some aviation teams that performed at different events, although the teams did not have a formal name or message.

At the end of World War II, the US armed services were in a state of flux. Even though the US Navy was downsizing after the war, the Navy still needed personnel to support their carrier fleet and aircraft in peacetime. It remained a challenge to encourage young men to join the Navy, particularly men from interior parts of the country, away from the coasts. Therefore, in 1946 the Navy decided that one such vehicle to promote enlistment into the Navy was to promote naval aviation, and thus the idea of a flight exhibition team to perform in public came about.

The idea started in the US Navy public-affairs office, and an experienced aviator, Lt. Cdr. Roy "Butch" Voris, was chosen to head this team. He was put in charge of selecting men and putting together the team in Jacksonville, Florida, with a goal of having the team ready by June 1946. In addition, he selected the Grumman F6F Hellcat, a major aircraft used during World War II, for the team, .

The team first flew in public on June 15, 1946, in Jacksonville, Florida, followed by visits to other states in the middle of the country.

In the beginning, the term "Flight Exhibition Team" was used, and eventually, through various naming contests, it was narrowed down to Blue Lancers or Blue Angels, with the latter being somewhat inspired by the name of a nightclub in New York. The name gained popularity and has been used ever since, for the last seventy years.

The evolution of Blue Angels aircraft mirrors the advances of aviation over the seventy years—going from propeller-driven aircraft to the current jet engines currently used by the team.

The Blue Angels fly throughout the US each year and, in a two-year period, will cover over 100 different locations in the US before returning to the same locations again. When the Angels arrive at a location, it is a major event to the airport and surrounding community where they are based, and various public-relations events are arranged.

The mission of the Blue Angels is to showcase the pride and professionalism of the US Navy and Marine Corps by inspiring a culture of excellence and service to country through flight demonstration and community outreach.

BLUE ANGELS AIRCRAFT MODELS

Model	Years in Team
Grumman F6F-5 Hellcat	1946
Grumman F8F-1 Bearcat	1946–1952
Grumman F9F-2, F9F-5 Panther	1949–1954
Grumman F9F-8 Cougar	1955–1957
Grumman F11F-1 Tiger (short nose)	1957–1958
Grumman F11F-1 Tiger (long nose)	1959–1968
McDonnell Douglas F-4J Phantom	1969–1973
Douglas A-4F Skyhawk II	1974–1986
Boeing F/A-18C/D	1987 to present

The Blue Angels crest was developed in 1949 by
Lt. Cmdr. Raleigh Rhodes. It features the four-
aircraft diamond formation and the Naval Air
Training Command (NATC) emblem. *US Navy*

CHAPTER 1

Grumman F6F Hellcat

The F6F Hellcat was a carrier-based aircraft used by the US Navy in World War II, and it would be the first aircraft used by the Navy exhibition team in 1946.

Team leader Butch Voris had the aircraft painted in US Navy colors: blue and gold. Maneuvers performed by the team consisted of three-aircraft "V" patterns, loops, and inverted flight passes. Since the war ended only a year before, the crowds were entertained by simulated dogfights between the team and an SNJ trainer painted in yellow to resemble a Japanese Zero.

The F6F Hellcats flew shows in Florida and in several midwestern states. They were used by the team only for a short time until August 1946, when the team would transition to Grumman F8F Bearcat.

This is an early photo of the Blue Angels F6F Hellcats in formation. The aircraft were painted Navy Blue with yellow numbers on the vertical tail section. The team used the F6F Bearcat for a short time so photos for this aircraft are rare. *US Navy*

F6F HELLCAT SPECIFICATIONS

Wingspan	42 feet, 10 inches
Length	33 feet, 7 inches
Height	13 feet, 1 inches.
Empty weight	9,042 pounds
Power plant	One Pratt &Whitney R-2800-10W radial engine
Maximum speed	376 mph
Service ceiling	37,500 feet
Range	1,090 miles

A total of 12,275 F6F Hellcats were built for the US Navy, and it was the major fighter used against the Japanese "Zero" aircraft in the Pacific during World War II. The Hellcat was credited with destroying over 5,200 Japanese aircraft and served with the US Navy until 1954. *US Navy*

CHAPTER 2

Grumman F8F Bearcat

F8F BEARCAT SPECIFICATIONS

Wingspan	35 feet, 10 inches
Length	28 feet, 3 inches
Height	13 feet, 10 inches.
Empty weight	7,070 pounds
Power plant	One Pratt & Whitney R-2800-34W radial engine
Maximum speed	421 mph
Service ceiling	40,000 feet
Range	1,105 miles

A total of 1,265 F8F Bearcats were manufactured for the US Navy and served until 1952. *US Navy*

Grumman performed all modification work on the Blue Angels F8F Bearcat aircraft in their factory in Bethpage, New York, in 1946. The team would pick up these aircraft in August 1946 and begin using them the following year. *Northrop Grumman History Center*

The F8F Bearcat succeeded the F6F Hellcat in US Navy service, and the Hellcats used by the Blue Angels as well. The Bearcat began production in 1945, missing World War II, and was in US Navy service until 1952. It would become a popular plane that was used in civilian aircraft racing into the 1960s.

The Blue Angels flew the Bearcat from 1946 through 1952, with a short break in 1951, when flying was suspended because Blue Angels pilots were called back into active US service during the Korean War in 1950 and 1951. The team would reach levels of fifty shows in a single year, such as in 1949.

Different maneuvers would be developed for airshows, such as dives and some unusual moves, the latter including one known as the "rope trick" in which the aircraft were tied together by rope. It was during the F8F tenure with the Angels that maneuvers such as the Diamond Loop and the Diamond Barrel Roll was developed, and these are still part of the team's repertoire to this day.

There would be a total of sixteen different Bearcat serial numbers (Bureau Numbers, or BuNos) used in Blue Angels service, with one aircraft lost in September 1946, shortly after the team received the Bearcat.

The team is in front of their new Bearcat at the Grumman facility in Bethpage. Team lead is Butch Voris, who is second from the right, along with members May, Wickendoll, and Knight.
Northrop Grumman History Center

CHAPTER 3

Grumman F9F-5 Panther

F9F-5 PANTHER SPECIFICATIONS

Wingspan	38 feet
Length	37 feet, 5 inches
Height	11 feet, 4 inches.
Empty weight	10,147 pounds
Power plant	One Pratt & Whitney J42-P-6/P-8 turbojet engine
Maximum speed	579 mph
Service ceiling	42,800 feet
Range	1,300 miles

A total of 1,382 F9F Panthers were built for the US Navy. The aircraft was one of the earliest jets used by the Navy and featured fold-up wings for better storage on aircraft carrier decks. *US Navy*

An early color shot shows the core-four aircraft of the Blue Angels Panther team flying in formation, with the #1 aircraft in the lead. The leader of the Blue Angels during this time was Butch Voris again, at the request of the Navy. *Northrop Grumman History Center*

The F9F Panther was the entry of the Blue Angels team into the jet age. The use of jet engines would require a change to the team's routine in which the jet aircraft would have to fly farther away from the crowds, in comparison to the propeller-driven F8F. Also, certain maneuvers such as the "rope trick," where the aircraft were tied together, had to be deleted from the show

The team initially trained with the F9F-2 Panthers from 1949 through a portion of 1950 while still flying the F8F Bearcat in shows. By 1950, Blue Angels pilots were called back into active US service during Korean War in 1950 and 1951. After war activity slowed down, the team would fly F9F-5 Panthers, beginning in June 1952 and continuing through 1954.

During 1953, there was an evaluation of six F9F-6 Cougars that were loaned to the show, but they were not incorporated into the team at that time due to various performance issues. Each version had design improvements over the previous version.

Eighteen different F9F Panther serial numbers were used during the service of this model with the Blue Angels, with the loss of two aircraft.

There were some mechanical issues experienced on the Panther that delayed the team's schedule until June 1952, after the return of pilots from Korea. *Northrop Grumman History Center*

Blue Angels #1 to #4 in a basic echelon formation, with #1 leading. *US Navy*

Blue Angels #1 to #4 fly in a modified diamond formation, where #1 is in the front and highest and #4 is in the back and the lowest. *US Navy*

With the F-9 Cougar jet, the team could move away from maneuvers that were developed for the early propeller-driven aircraft into different formations that showcased the jet's capabilities. *US Navy*

The team was starting to develop more formal and structured formations for the airshows where it performed. Here is an early version of the F9F Panthers flying in the echelon formation. *US Navy*

Blue Angels from the 1953 team are in the foreground with the F9F Panther in the background in this publicity photo. *US Navy*

Maintenance crew take a break in 1949 while #1 F9F Panther is being refueled at the tip tanks at the end of the wings. *US Navy*

Blue Angels #1 F9F-5 aircraft has just experienced a runway mishap in July 1952, and personnel are moving it. *US Navy*

The 1952 team is walking past their F9F Panther aircraft in Jacksonville, Florida, in December 1952. The team consisted of (*left to right*) Buddy Rich, Pat Murphy, Ray Hawkins, Cmdr. Butch Voris, and Frank Graham (the team's information officer). Voris had survived a midair collision with another Blue Angels aircraft earlier in the year, during an airshow in Corpus Christi, Texas, in July 1952, in which that pilot Dwight Wood was killed. Voris would serve as leader of the team until 1953. *National Archives*

During 1952, when the Angels were assigned the F9F-5 Panthers, they were requested by the US Navy to evaluate the Vought F7U Cutlass for incorporation into the team's airshow routine. The aircraft would not fly in formation with the Panthers, due to a number of issues. *US Navy*

In 1952, two F7U aircraft (BuNos 124426 and 124427) were assigned to the Blue Angels team for evaluation and were actually assigned #7 on the tail. Since the F7U had both performances and maintenance issues, it would be discontinued from the team before the end of 1952. *US Navy*

CHAPTER 4

Grumman F9F-8 Cougar

F9F-8 COUGAR SPECIFICATIONS	
Wingspan	36 feet, 4 inches
Length	42 feet, 7 inches
Height	15 feet
Empty weight	13,000 pounds
Power plant	One Pratt & Whitney J48-P-8A turbojet engine
Maximum speed	690 mph
Service ceiling	50,500 feet
Range	1,000 miles

The F9F Cougar was a carrier-based aircraft for the US Navy. A total of 1,988 F9F-8 Cougars were built by Grumman. Here is an early production model conducting flight testing over eastern Long Island. *Northrop Grumman History Center*

The main instrument console for the US Navy F9F Cougar was the same for the Blue Angels F9F. The gun-firing button on the control stick was deactivated for the Blue Angels aircraft. *Grumman archives via Cradle of Aviation Museum*

The F9F Cougar was powered by a single Pratt & Whitney J48-P-8A turbojet engine. *Ken Neubeck*

The F9F Cougar was the swept-wing version of the F9F Panther, and it was the first swept-wing jet aircraft that the Blue Angels would use. The aircraft was officially used by the Blue Angels team from 1955 through 1957. There was an initial evaluation of six aircraft made in the F9F-6 version of the Cougar, which was conducted by the team in 1953. However, there were mechanical issues that resulted and the aircraft was returned to the factory and then into fleet service. In the meantime, the team continued flying the F9F Panther model.

In late 1954, the team conducted transition training into the F9F-8 version of the Cougar, with 1955 being the launch year for airshows of this model. It was at this point that additional maneuvers were incorporated into the show, including the six-aircraft delta formation, a staple formation used to the current time.

A total of thirteen different BuNos for the F9F Cougars were used by the team. There were no major incidents or fatalities during the short time that the team flew Cougars.

Blue Angels F9F Cougars are being serviced by maintenance personnel during an airshow visit, circa 1955. *Northrop Grumman History Center*

Publicity photo shows the core four members of the team in nose-to-nose arrangement, along with the wings being folded up. Team leader Cdr. Ed Holley is seen waving from his aircraft in the lower right. *Northrop Grumman History Center*

Blue Angels Cougars main four aircraft are in line abreast formation. The era of swept-wing jet aircraft for the team has begun. *Northrop Grumman History Center*

Blue Angels F9F Cougars #1 through #4 are in the diamond formation. *Cradle of Aviation Museum*

Blue Angels F9F Cougars #1 through #4 are in the echelon parade formation. *Cradle of Aviation Museum*

Blue Angels F9F Cougars #1 through #4 are in the echelon parade formation. Although the single-seat Cougar had a short service with the team, the two-seat Cougar would serve with the team for several more years as the #7 media aircraft. *Northrop Grumman History Center*

CHAPTER 5
Grumman F11F Tiger

F11F TIGER SPECIFICATIONS	
Wingspan	31 feet, 7.5 inches
Length	46 feet, 11 inches
Height	13 feet, 3 inches.
Empty weight	13,810 pounds
Power plant	One Wright J65-W-18A turbojet engine
Maximum speed	727 mph
Service ceiling	49,000 feet
Range	1,275 miles

The F11F (later designated as F-11) would be the second-longest-tenured aircraft model used by the Blue Angels, beginning in 1957 and continuing until the team went to the F-4 in 1968. The F11F had only four years of operational history with the US Navy but would have more years of service time with the Blue Angels.

The F11F Tigers would be a major step up for the history of the Blue Angels. The Tiger brought increased performance capabilities over the Cougar with regard to speed (it was supersonic) and service ceiling. With the Tiger being with the Angels for such a long time, there were many more publicity photos that were taken of the team than there were with other models, with visits to major US cities and national landmarks.

Over forty-five different F11F serial numbers were used during the service of this model for the Blue Angels, representing over 23 percent of the entire F11F production run of 199 aircraft. There were seven Tigers with six pilots killed due to accidents during service with this aircraft.

The Blue Angels F11F Tiger was the first to fly outside the country, including stops in Europe, Mexico, and the Caribbean. When the F11F was retired from Blue Angels service in 1968, it would be the last Grumman-manufactured aircraft used by the Angels, ending a twenty-year run of Grumman aircraft used by the team.

In 1973, four years after the last F-11 flew as a member of the Blue Angels, two ex–Blue Angels F-11 Tigers (BuNos 141824 and 141853) were brought out of storage from the "boneyard" located at Davis-Monthan AFB for a special evaluation. This evaluation was for testing the concept of in-flight thrust reversers.

The program was to evaluate the concept of an in-flight thrust reverser proposed by the Rohr Corporation that would allow an aircraft to convert 100 percent of its forward thrust into 50 percent thrust in the opposite direction in less than two seconds. Such a device had tactical applications that would change tactical maneuvering, dive angles for the release of ordnance along infrared suppression capability. The thrust reverser was manufactured by Rohr Industries, with Grumman performing aircraft modification and repainting.

The two aircraft were in Blue Angels paint scheme and were converted to a white paint scheme with red trim and special markings. BuNo 141853 was designated as the #1 aircraft and was modified with a 33-inch tail extension on the tail section. BuNo 141824 was left in original Tiger configuration and would serve as the chase aircraft.

Flight testing was conducted by Grumman test pilots at the Calverton facility in Long Island during the summer of 1974, and after the initial test flights the two aircraft were handed over to US Navy test pilots at Pax River in the fall of 1974.

At the conclusion of testing, both Tigers were officially retired, with the flight-reverser Tiger ending up in the Pueblo Museum and the chase Tiger being sent to the Pima Air & Space Museum. The latter aircraft was restored to its original Blue Angels colors by the museum.

The program was strictly a one-off test to evaluate the effectiveness of the flight reverser and was not meant to bring the Tiger back into active duty or to be used for any other tests. It was convenient that Tiger aircraft were available and could be brought back to flightworthy condition. Recommendations were made that a more modern US Navy aircraft such as the F-14 be used to conduct further evaluations of the flight-reverser design, but this did not happen.

The flight-reverser program would officially be the last hurrah for the F-11 Tiger, putting a final touch on the unusual service career of this aircraft. The thrust-reverser program is an interesting sidebar with regard to the history of the Blue Angels.

A total of 199 F11F Tigers were built. The aircraft served the US Navy from 1958 through 1961 but was withdrawn from US Navy carrier service due to performance issues of the aircraft and reliability issues concerning the engine. The Blue Angels would use this aircraft for much longer.
Northrop Grumman Historical Center

The cockpit for the F11F Tiger was identical both for the operational model and the Blue Angels model, with some minor modifications. This included the deletion of the guns and controls associated with the guns. *Northrop Grumman Historical Center*

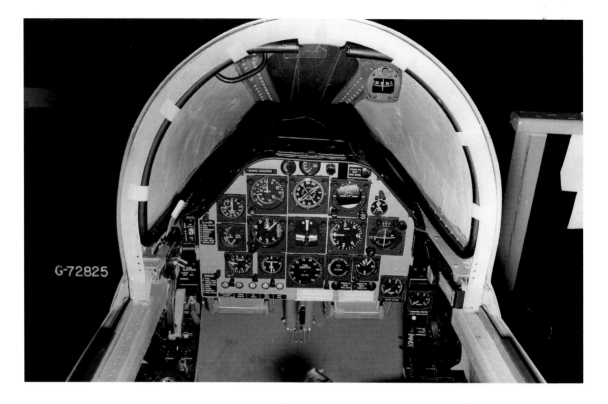

The engine used in the F11F Tiger was the Wright J65-W-18A turbojet engine, which, despite having reliability problems, served the team well for over ten years. *Northrop Grumman History Center*

The first set of F11F Tigers used by the Blue Angels was the "short-nose version," which the team flew from 1957 through 1958. The aircraft has a short nose, with the distinctive refueling probe located on the nose. A total of ten different BuNos for these short-nose aircraft were used by the team during the time that the planes flew with the team. The first three photos show the standard diamond and echelon formations involving aircraft #1 through #4, and the last photo shows the introduction of solo maneuvers by aircraft #5 and #6. *Cradle of Aviation Museum*

For a two-year period, from 1957 through 1958, the team flew the short-nose Tigers, seen here flying in the echelon formation. *US Navy photo via Cradle of Aviation*

From 1959 through 1968, the team flew the long-nose Tigers, seen here in the diamond formation.
US Navy photo via Cradle of Aviation

The 1958 Blue Angels team in front of the #6 Tiger (*left to right*): Lt. John Damian, Lt. Bob Rasmussen, Lt. Herb Hunter, Capt. Stoney Mayock, Cmdr. Ed Holley (leader), and Lt. Jack Dewenter. *US Navy photo via Northrop Grumman History Center*

The same 1958 Blue Angels team is shown here standing by the tail of the F11F Tiger, which was the short-nose F11F Tiger version at that time. *US Navy photo via Northrop Grumman History Center*

The 1961 Blue Angels team in front of the #1 Tiger (*left to right*): Lt. Dan MacIntyre, Marine Capt. Doug McCougher, Cmdr. Zeb Knott (team leader), Lt. Bill Rennie, Lt. Cmdr. Ken Wallace, and Lt. Lou Charham.
Northrop Grumman History Center

The 1961 Blue Angels team again, in a different photo opportunity. By this time, the team was flying the long-nose F11F Tiger version. *Northrop Grumman History Center*

The full complement of six F11F Blue Angels Tigers is preparing for a show. *Northrop Grumman History Center*

Maintenance crew are at attention in front of their assigned aircraft, preparing for pilots to approach and enter their aircraft. *Northrop Grumman History Center*

This is a rare photo of all six Blue Angels F11F aircraft in the delta formation during takeoff from Calverton on Long Island. *Cradle of Aviation Museum*

Blue Angels #5 and #6 perform maneuvers over Rocky Mountain. *Cradle of Aviation Museum*

Blue Angels F11F #1 through #4 are seen here in the diamond formation. Many of the publicity photos from this time period show just the first four aircraft. *Northrop Grumman History Center*

Blue Angels F11F #1 through #4 are seen here during preflight procedures at North Island, California, in 1962. *US Navy*

AIR SHOW/OPEN HOUSE

OCTOBER 21-22, 1967

PERFECTION through and PRIDE
PROFESSIONALISM
NAVAL AIR STATION
NEW ORLEANS

Blue Angels
J. W. Bill Fornof
Operation Recovery
Wayne Flickinger
Navy Relief Prizes
Navy Art
NAS Model Airplane Team
NASA Displays

Flying Professor
Golden Knights
Tom Jacomini
Bill Cochran
Radio Control Models
Static Aircraft
SeaBee Exhibit
Model Airplanes

NAVAL AIR STATION

New Orleans, Louisiana

This is a flyer for an airshow that the Angels participated in at the Naval Air Station in New Orleans. Inside the flyer is a photo of four Blue Angels F11F aircraft performing the diamond vertical-break procedure shown at right.

Four Blue Angels F11F aircraft are performing the diamond vertical-break procedure. The procedure involves Blue Angels #1 through #4 climbing vertically in the diamond pattern, with #1 in the lead. At the determined altitude, the four aircraft split into four different directions. *US Navy photo via Northrop Grumman History Center*

The F11F Tiger would serve in the US Navy for only four years, while the Blue Angels team used it for over twelve years.

Blue Angels F11F #1 through #4 are in diamond formation in one of their many photo opportunities as they pass by the Statue of Liberty in New York City. *Cradle of Aviation Museum*

Blue Angels F11F #1 through #4 are in diamond formation as they pass the United Nations Building and the Empire State Building in Midtown Manhattan. *Cradle of Aviation Museum*

Blue Angels F11F #1 through #4 in diamond formation as they pass over Niagara Falls. *Cradle of Aviation Museum*

Blue Angels F11F #1 through #4 in diamond formation as they pass by Mount Rushmore in South Dakota. The team is trailing red, white, and blue smoke for the occasion. *Cradle of Aviation Museum*

Blue Angels F11F #1 through #4 in diamond formation as they pass over the Golden Gate Bridge in San Francisco. The bridge would continue to be a popular photo opportunity for the team over the next forty years. *Northrop Grumman History Center*

Lt. Bill Rennie is flying Blue Angels #6 in 1961. He would fly with the Angels for two years, and during his twenty-year Navy career, he accrued over 4,800 flying hours. *Cradle of Aviation Museum*

CHAPTER 6
McDonnell Douglas F-4J Phantom

F-4J PHANTOM SPECIFICATIONS	
Wingspan	38 feet, 5 inches
Length	63 feet
Height	16 feet, 5 inches.
Empty weight	30,328 pounds
Power plant	Two GE J790GE017A turbojet engines
Maximum speed	1,473 mph
Service ceiling	60,000 feet
Range	1,245 miles

The F11F Tiger had served the Blue Angels team well, but the aircraft went out of production in 1959, and it was not possible to get parts and support for the Tiger anymore. So a replacement was needed.

Different aircraft models were looked at by the team, including the A-4 Skyhawk, but this aircraft was needed for the Vietnam War. Because the Air Force Thunderbird team was getting the F-4 Phantom, the Blue Angels were able to get this model too, since there were six earlier models used during qualifications that were no longer needed by the Navy. These aircraft were modified with lead ballast in the nose rather than the guns, so this fit well for the team.

The F-4J Phantom was the first non-Grumman-manufactured aircraft used by the Blue Angels team. It started performing in 1969, and besides doing airshows in the US, it went outside the country, including a tour in Southeast Asia, visiting the Philippines, Taiwan, and Korea in 1971. In 1973, the team visited Europe (France, Spain, and Italy) and the Middle East (Iran and Turkey).

The F-4 Phantom was almost double the speed of the predecessor F11F Tiger, and this allowed for more capabilities during airshow performances. For example, it took longer for the F11F aircraft to reach the airspeed required for some maneuvers, whereas the F-4 aircraft could accomplish this in less time.

Unfortunately, there were a number of crashes involving the F-4J aircraft with the team during the five-year service, including two separate midair collisions resulting in crashes during 1973. The first took place in March, when three aircraft collided during practice in El Centro, California, and all pilots ejected safety. The second event took place during a preshow practice flight in Lakehurst, New Jersey, on July 26, when two aircraft collided, killing three team members. The balance of the season was canceled.

During the F-4J years, ten of fourteen aircraft were lost, along with four crew members losing their lives. This was a low point in the history of the Angels team, with the crashes, low public opinion regarding the military, and the ongoing fuel crisis in the US.

F-4J PHANTOM BLUE ANGELS AIRCRAFT CRASHES

Date	Location	BuNo	Description	Fatal Casualties
November 6, 1969	El Paso, Texas	153075	Ran out of fuel	No
August 30, 1970	Cedar Rapids, Iowa	153054	Gear-up landing	No
June 4, 1971	Quonset, Rhode Island	153082	In-flight fire	No
February 14, 1972	Superstition Mountains, Arizona	153086	Crash during practice	Yes (1)
March 8, 1973	El Centro, California	153079	Midair collision during practice	No
March 8, 1973	El Centro, California	153080	Midair collision during practice	No
March 8, 1973	El Centro, California	153083	Midair collision during practice	No
July 6, 1973	Lake Charles, Louisiana	153876	Crash	No
July 26, 1973	Lakehurst, New Jersey	153072	Midair collision during practice	Yes (1)
July 26, 1973	Lakehurst, New Jersey	153081	Midair collision during practice	Yes (2)

The McDonnell Douglas F-4 Phantom II first flew in 1959 and served both for the US Navy and USAF. It saw significant action in the Vietnam War. Over 5,195 F-4s were built, with some still in foreign service today. *US Navy*

The F-4 Phantom Blue Angels did several tours outside the US, into Asia and Europe. Here the team is shown performing maneuvers in Puerto Rico. *US Navy*

The F-4 Phantom Blue Angels are seen here doing a landing-gear-down maneuver, which slows the aircraft down during flight. *US Navy*

During its short service career with the Blue Angels, the team traveled to locations outside the US, including parts of Europe and Asia. The Blue Angels F-4 are shown here in Puerto Rico. *US Navy*

Most of the F-4 Blue Angels maneuvers performed during the airshow worked off the four-aircraft diamond formation. *US Navy*

Blue Angels are in standard four-aircraft diamond formation. Note the dummy air-to-air missiles mounted underneath each aircraft. *US Navy*

CHAPTER 7
McDonnell Douglas
A-4F Skyhawk

A-4F SKYHAWK SPECIFICATIONS

Wingspan	26 feet, 6 inches
Length	40 feet, 3 inches
Height	15 feet
Empty weight	10,450 pounds
Power plant	One Pratt & Whitney J52-P8A turbojet engine
Maximum speed	673 mph
Service ceiling	42,250 feet
Range	2,000 miles

The McDonnell Douglas A-4 Skyhawk was used exclusively by the US Navy. Over 2,960 A-4s were built. *US Navy*

The Blue Angels Skyhawk team at El Centro, California. This location served as the winter location for the Blue Angels, where they would perform their training prior to the start of an airshow season. *US Navy Photo by PHAN Pat Smith*

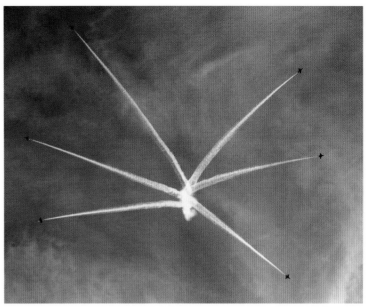

The Blue Angels A-4 team is performing a bomb burst maneuver in 1984, which is made effective by the use of smoke. *US Navy photo by PH2 Paul O' Mara*

In late 1973, the Blue Angels were assigned the McDonnell Douglas A-4F Skyhawk to replace the F-4 Phantom. The Angels would be going from a twin-engine F-4 to a single engine A-4 aircraft that was lighter and slower than the F-4. The Angels began training on the aircraft for the 1974 season.

The A-4 Skyhawk was a carrier-based aircraft that was introduced into US Navy and US Marine service, beginning in 1956. The Skyhawk was used in the squadrons until 1979 and was used after that as a training aircraft into the 1990s. It saw significant action during the early years of Vietnam as the main carrier-based attack aircraft for the US Navy.

The Blue Angels did extensive training on this aircraft, with the knowledge that they had to move on past the difficulties encountered with the F-4 Phantom. Certain maneuvers were not used by the team right away, until everything was worked out.

The Blue Angels flew the Skyhawk from 1974 through 1986. It was during this period that the shows were defined as high, low, or flat. This protocol continues to the present time. All shows performed by the A-4 were confined to the United States. Over eighteen different A-4F BuNos were used during this time, and six aircraft were lost due to accidents.

Special 35th Anniversary artwork showing the original Blue Angel F6F Hellcat and the Blue Angels A-4 Skyhawk. *McDonnell Douglas via Mike Machat*

Blue Angels #1 through #4 are landing in diamond formation, with #5 and #6 in the distant sky following behind. *US Navy photo by PH2 Paul O' Mara*

Blue Angels #5 is conducting a landing approach with all landing gears and wing flaps extended. *US Navy photo by PH2 Paul O' Mara*

Blue Angels perform the "fleur-de-lis" maneuver in 1984. *US Navy*

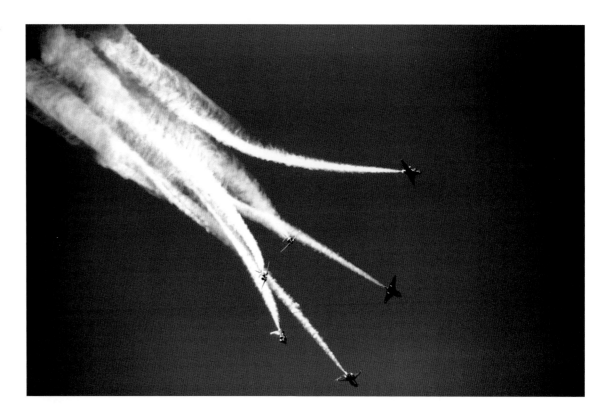

Blue Angels #6, BuNo 154172, piloted by Lt. Andy Caputi, is conducting a low-level pass above the runway, with landing gear up. *US Navy photo by PH2 Paul O' Mara*

This is an underside view of six Blue Angels A-4F aircraft flying in the standard delta formation. *US Navy*

Five Blue Angels are flying in delta formation in July 1984 during a practice run near the waters in Florida. *US Navy photo by PH2 Paul O' Mara*

Six Blue Angels A-4s are flying in formation with landing gears fully extended during a synchronized team landing at an airshow in Florida in 1984. *US Navy photo by PH2 Paul O'Mara*

Six Blue Angels A-4s are flying in the delta formation in 1984. *US Navy photo by PH2 Paul O'Mara*

Blue Angels are in the process of performing the "fleur-de-lis" maneuver, in which aircraft #1 through #4 fly in one direction toward inverted flight formation as the #5 and #6 aircraft peel off into a different direction to do inverted flight as well. *US Navy photo by PH2 Paul O'Mara*

Blue Angels aircraft #1 through #4 are in the echelon right formation during a flyby pass over the crowds during an airshow in 1984. *US Navy photo by PH2 Paul O'Mara*

In 1984, Blue Angels aircraft #5 and #6 pass each other in an opposing solo routine known as opposing knife edge. *US Navy photo by PH2 Paul O'Mara*

Another routine involving Blue Angels aircraft #5 and #6 is the Fortus maneuver, which gives a mirror-image effect to the spectators. *US Navy*

The Blue Angels Skyhawks did a number of publicity photos similar to what was done with the F11F Tiger. Here is the team flying in formation over the US Naval Academy in Annapolis, MD. *US Navy*

The team performs a high-speed delta formation movement with generated smoke coming from the A-4 Skyhawks in July 1984. *US Navy photo by OH2 Paul O' Mara*

The Blue Angels Skyhawks are doing a flyby in delta formation in front of Mount Rushmore in South Dakota, a national monument that the Blue Angels Tigers visited for a photo shoot some years earlier. *US Navy*

CHAPTER 8
Boeing F/A-18C/D Hornet

F/A-18C HORNET SPECIFICATIONS	
Wingspan	37 feet, 5 inches
Length	56 feet, 1 inch
Height	15 feet, 5 inches
Empty weight	23,000 pounds
Power plant	Two GE F404-GE-402 turbofan engines
Maximum speed	1,190 mph
Service ceiling	50,000 feet
Range	2,071 miles

The Boeing F/A-18 Hornet has been used by the US Navy since 1983, and with the Blue Angels since 1987. This Hornet is a US Navy aircraft painted in special colors, celebrating the centennial of US naval aviation in 2011. *Ken Neubeck*

The photos above show that in addition to the team releaseing smoke during the actual airshow, that individual aircraft will release smoke during a practice run, prior to landing. *Ken Neubeck*

In late 1986, the Blue Angels were assigned the F/A-18C (single-seat) and F/A-18D (two-seat) aircraft to begin training on the planes for the 1987 season, and these have been flown by the team up to the current time.

The F-18 was a carrier-based aircraft that was introduced into US Navy and US Marine Corps service beginning in 1983. The Hornet has seen significant operational history with the US, including Operation Desert Storm, Afghanistan, and other actions to the present day.

The F/A-18 Hornet is the second Blue Angels model to have two engines since the F-4 Phantom in 1973. The aircraft is larger than the A-4 Skyhawk, since it is twice the weight. Its top speed is hundreds of miles per hour faster than the Skyhawk, providing more thrust when needed. This allows the team to execute the various maneuvers during the show at a faster pace and with more precision. With the Hornet, the training is more intense for the pilots when upgrading to this type of aircraft.

Highlights for the F/A-18's time with the team include the 1992 trip to Europe, the first overseas trip for the team since 1973. Countries visited have included Russia, Sweden, Finland, and England, among others.

Over the thirty-year period to date, over sixty different BuNos of the F/A-18 aircraft have been used by the team. During the period that the Blue Angels have been flying the Hornet, the accident rate has been low, with just six incidents occurring, and only one during the past ten years, in 2016.

The #7 aircraft is an F/A18D model that has two cockpit stations, in which the two Blue Angels pilots associated with the public-relations aspect of the airshow sit in. The front cockpit station is similar to the single-seat cockpit station of the other single-seat Blue Angels aircraft. In this view, it can be seen that the wing tip area is a yellow-painted rail structure, in place of where a bomb rack for a missile would be used in an active F/A-18 Hornet aircraft. *Ken Neubeck*

The front cockpit section consists of two digital displays on the left and right that surround a up-front control panel. There is a Heads-Up Display (HUD) on top of the console, and a timer clock above the control panel. *Ken Neubeck*

The rear cockpit section is identical to the front cockpit section, except that there is no HUD or clock. This is the seat for the media member to sit during the media flight. *Ken Neubeck*

F/A-18 Hornet used by the Blue Angels have been modified in several areas from the Navy Hornet. One is that the M61 Vulcan machine gun in the nose cone has been replaced with a special tank that holds smoke oil. The paraffin-based oil in the tank is injected into the plane's exhaust nozzles, instantly vaporizing it and creating the smoke trails used in the show. *Ken Neubeck*

Maintenance crew are filling the special tank in the forward fuselage with the smoke oil that will be used to create smoke for a performance in July 2012. Biodegradable, paraffin-based oil is injected through a special nozzle into the exhaust plume where the oil is instantly vaporized into thick smoke.
US Navy photo by MCS 1st Class Rachel McMarr

Another special feature of the Blue Angels F/A-18 Hornet is that a high-gloss, low-friction paint is applied to the fuselage of the aircraft to reduce drag, thus helping the aircraft to perform high-level maneuvers. *Ken Neubeck*

The surface of the high-gloss paint on the Hornet is so smooth that it is able to reflect like a mirror, as seen here with the reflection of the sun rising on the forward fuselage. *Ken Neubeck*

The pilots of the Blue Angels Hornet do not wear G suits. A G suit includes inflating and deflating air bladders that would interfere with the pilot controlling the aircraft. Thus, pilots learn body exercises such as clenching their stomach and leg muscles to prevent blood from rushing from their heads to their lower extremities, which could cause blackouts.
Ken Neubeck

The control stick of the Blue Angels Hornet has had a small spring installed that applies forty pounds of nose-down pressure, which makes it easier for the aircraft to fly in formation as well as being able to fly in inverted flight. Each individual pilot adapts to this load in graduated steps during the winter training period at El Centro, California. *US Navy photo by PH1 Casey Akins*

The F/A-18 aircraft is the most powerful aircraft ever flown by the Blue Angels. The aircraft is powered by a pair of General Electric F404-GE-402 turbofan engines. *Ken Neubeck*

This is the F404-GE-402 turbofan engine being tested on the maintenance deck of the USS *Dwight D. Eisenhower* (CVN-69). *US Navy photo by MCS 3rd Class Nathan Parde*

The nose landing gear for the F/A-18 has a launch bar extension that is able to be attached to the steam catapult mechanism for launching on aircraft carriers. *Ken Neubeck*

The main landing-gear struts for the F/A-18 have a kneeling configuration, with the actuator situated in the rear of the struts. *Ken Neubeck*

The planes may change, but the aircraft will always be in the classic formation from #1 through #6 when parked on the tarmac during any event. *Ken Neubeck*

The Blue Angels follow strict formation in every aspect of their performance. Here, after a practice run in 2018, the team is going down the runway in groups of two aircraft as they approach their assigned spot on the tarmac and their maintenance crew. *Ken Neubeck*

This Blue Angels #1 aircraft was flown in 2016 by the leader, in this case Cmdr. Ryan Bernacchi, who led the team in 2016 and 2017. The #1 aircraft is often referred to as the "Boss." *Ken Neubeck*

This Blue Angels #2 aircraft was flown in 2016 by the right wingman, Lt. Matt Suyderhoud, who flew with the team in 2015 and 2016. *Ken Neubeck*

This Blue Angels #3 aircraft was flown in 2016 by the left wingman, Lt. Lance Benson, who flew with the team in 2016 and 2017. *Ken Neubeck*

This Blue Angels #4 aircraft was flown in 2016 by the left wingman, Lt. Andy Talbot, who flew with the team in 2015 and 2016. This aircraft is landing at Republic Aiport in Long Island, NY, with the airport control tower seen in the background. *Ken Neubeck*

This Blue Angels #5 aircraft was flown in 2016 by lead solo Lt. Ryan Chamberlain, who flew with the team in 2015 and 2016 in this position but had previously flown the #7 aircraft in 2014 as the public-relations officer. *Ken Neubeck*

This is the Blue Angels #6 aircraft flown by Lt. Brandon Hempler coming in for a landing in May 2018. *Ken Neubeck*

The Blue Angels team performs different group configurations during the practice round of airshow week. Here is a three-aircraft delta formation consisting of aircraft #1, #2, and #4, which just released smoke prior to landing at Republic Airport in May 2018. *Ken Neubeck*

While maintenance personnel work on preparing a single-seat F/A-18C Hornet for upcoming run as well as changing the number of the aircraft, a Geico Skytyper T-6 Texan is taking off from the runway at Republic Airport. There will typically be a number of other aerobatic performers at airshows, with the Blue Angels team being the grand finale. *Ken Neubeck*

Aircraft #1 and #2 touch down and land together side by side on the runway after a practice run performed in Long Island, with contrails streaming off the wings.
Ken Neubeck

Blue Angels F/A-18 Hornets #1 through #5 make their initial arrival in Long Island by flying in the modified delta formation for five aircraft and releasing smoke over Republic Airport in May 2018.
Ken Neubeck

From the delta formation, the aircraft break out in different directions, with #1 pulling up to be the first in single-file aircraft landing for the team. *Ken Neubeck*

Blue Angels #1, flown by Capt. Greg McWherter, is being refueled over South Carolina on the way to Latrobe, Pennsylvania, for an airshow in June 2012. Whenever the team makes extended trips, aerial refueling is necessary. *US Navy photo by MCS 1st Class Rachel McMarr*

The entire Blue Angels team is being refueled by a Boeing KC-135 Stratotanker over Colorado in September 2012, during a cross-country trip. *US Navy photo by MCS 2nd Class Andrew Johnson*

The Blue Angels doing a delta formation pass for a photo opportunity during their regular visit to "Fleet Week" in San Francisco in October 2017. *US Navy photo by MCS 2nd Class Kory Alsberry*

The Blue Angels doing a six-aircraft delta formation pass during a photo opportunity over lower Manhattan, December 2013. The different cities that are visited mirror the cities visited by the Blue Angels F11F aircraft some fifty years earlier. *US Navy photo by MCS 1st Class Terrance Siren*

The Blue Angels doing a six-aircraft line abreast pass over Boston Harbor on July 4, 2012, during "Navy Week" there as part of the celebration of the War of 1812 bicentennial. *US Navy photo by MCS 3rd Class Billy Ho*

The Blue Angels are flying in standard delta formation along with eight Alpha jets in delta formation from the Patrouille Acrobatique de France aero team over Pensacola, Florida, in April 2017. *US Navy photo by MCS 3rd Class Dominick Cremeans*

CHAPTER 9
Support Aircraft and Crew

The R5D-3 transport was used by the Blue Angels during the Cougar and Phantom periods. The aircraft was painted in Blue Angels color and assigned the number "8," which was painted on the tail as seen on this R5D-2, BuNo 50868. *Northrop Grumman History Center*

As the Blue Angels team went to faster jets, such as the F9F and F11F aircraft, the need for additional maintenance support was needed concerning maintainers, parts, and support equipment. This drove the request for a transport-style aircraft to accompany the team during airshow events.

Beginning in 1949, the team was supported by a Douglas R5D-2, which was the case until the end of 1968. In 1968, when the Blue Angels were flying the F-4 Phantoms, they initially used a Lockheed C-121 Constellation transport aircraft to carry the maintenance personnel and support equipment. However, the "Connie" had limitations regarding the ability to unload equipment, because the cargo bay doors were 10 feet above the ground, requiring that a fork lift be available at each location that the Blue Angels team visited.

The commander of the team at the time, Bill Wheat, fought for the versatile Lockheed C-130 Hercules to be used, since it had cargo bay doors that opened to the ground, making it easier to load and unload equipment. By 1971 the C-130 was assigned to the team, and this aircraft type has been with the team since.

The C-130 is nicknamed "Fat Albert" and is flown by US Marine Corps pilots. The aircraft carries forty maintenance personnel for each show. The aircraft is an airshow performer as well, typically flying before the Blue Angels' jets performance, when it performs a number of maneuvers, including the famous sharp climb/bump during takeoff. While "Fat Albert" flies before the crowds, it collects weather information to feed back to the team. In addition, "Fat Albert" is used for conducting media flights, during which media personnel fly in the cargo area and the cockpit. The aircraft flies over 140,000 miles each season.

For a brief three-year period from 1968 through 1970, this Lockheed C-121 Constellation, BuNo 131623, was used as the transport aircraft for the Blue Angels when they were flying F-4J Phantoms. *US Navy*

A major problem with the team using the C-121 was that the access doors of the aircraft were located high above the ground and would require that forklifts be available to load and unload equipment from the aircraft, as can be seen in this photo. *US Navy*

The C-130 is a widely used aircraft that has been in US service since the 1950s. It is ideal for carrying equipment, parts, and maintenance personnel to different bases. The C-130 used by the Blue Angels is painted in the blue-and-yellow color scheme, but the aircraft does not show a number "8" on the tail, as was the case in previous transports used by the team. It is still considered as the #8 aircraft in the team. *Ken Neubeck*

The major difference in using the C-130 in lieu of the C-121 can be seen here: it has better loading and unloading features. A forklift can be used to unload and load equipment needed for maintenance during an event. *Ken Neubeck*

Located above the cabin entry door to the C-130 is the description "Fat Albert" Airlines, along with the names of the crew listed for the current Blue Angels season on the left side of the door. *Ken Neubeck*

US Marine captain Dusty Cook gives a quick tour of the cockpit area of "Fat Albert" during a media flight in 2016 in Long Island, New York. Note the large overhead control panel. Equipment and controls are the same as used in the standard C-130 aircraft used in service. *Ken Neubeck*

US Marine Corps captains Dusty Cook and A. J. Harrell, along with aircrew members, explain a few things to the media during a briefing in front of the cargo area of the "Fat Albert" C-130 during a Blue Angels visit to Republic Airport in Farmingdale, New York, in May 2014. *Ken Neubeck*

Aircrew members of "Fat Albert" C-130 look at the runway as they prepare to close the rear cargo doors during takeoff from Republic Airport. The aircraft is on the way to Fire Island during a media flight held in May 2014, where the team will perform as part of the Jones Beach Air Show. *Ken Neubeck*

With four engines powering the C-130, the aircraft is a very maneuverable aircraft that is able to perform sharp-angle takeoffs and landings along with sharp-angle banks. These maneuvers can create g-forces approaching 2 g, and during the takeoff hump, zero gravity can be experienced for a few seconds. *Ken Neubeck*

On occasion, when "Fat Albert" is down for repairs, an alternate C-130, BuNo 162310, nicknamed "Ernie," supports the Blue Angels team, as seen here for the 2012 Jones Beach Air Show event. *Ken Neubeck*

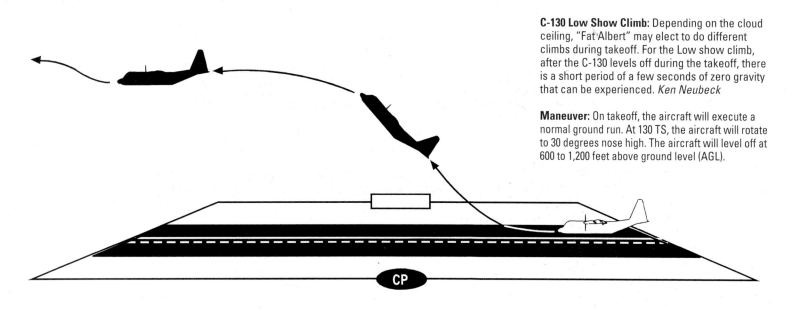

C-130 Low Show Climb: Depending on the cloud ceiling, "Fat Albert" may elect to do different climbs during takeoff. For the Low show climb, after the C-130 levels off during the takeoff, there is a short period of a few seconds of zero gravity that can be experienced. *Ken Neubeck*

Maneuver: On takeoff, the aircraft will execute a normal ground run. At 130 TS, the aircraft will rotate to 30 degrees nose high. The aircraft will level off at 600 to 1,200 feet above ground level (AGL).

CP

SPECTATOR AREA

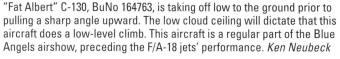

"Fat Albert" C-130, BuNo 164763, is taking off low to the ground prior to pulling a sharp angle upward. The low cloud ceiling will dictate that this aircraft does a low-level climb. This aircraft is a regular part of the Blue Angels airshow, preceding the F/A-18 jets' performance. *Ken Neubeck*

For a large aircraft, the Blue Angels C-130 is very maneuverable and can perform very steep dives, climbs and steep banking maneuvers. *Ken Neubeck*

Crew members in "Fat Albert" are hanging on to the ladder inside the cargo area as they experience weightlessness when the aircraft makes the sharp climb. *USAF photo by Staff Sgt. Ryan Crane*

For a number of years during airshows, the "Fat Albert" C-130 would conduct a short runway takeoff using jet-assisted takeoff (JATO), as demonstrated here in 2003. JATO was discontinued from the show in 2009 due to a shortage of rockets. *US Navy photo by Photographer's Mate 3rd Class Danielle L. Herlein*

However, "Fat Albert" C-130 has enough thrust in its engines that it is able to make takeoffs on short runways without JATO, as demonstrated here. *US Navy photo by Photographer's Mate 2nd Class Mark A. Ebert*

"Fat Albert" C-130 was pressed into active service during relief efforts due to Hurricane Ivan in September 2004. Note the blue-painted panels surrounding the gages and controls. *US Navy photo by Photographer's Mate 2nd Class Saul McSween*

Crew members from the "Fat Albert" C-130 are looking out the back cargo door during a photo mission of the Blue Angels team while training at El Centro, California, in March 2005. *US Navy photo by Photographer's Mate 2nd Class Saul McSween*

Maintenance support personnel is waiting for his assigned aircraft to arrive after conducting a practice run of the six aircraft at Republic Field, Long Island, in May 2016. *Ken Neubeck*

A Blue Angels aircraft has arrived, with pilot working with maintenance personnel prior to shutting down the aircraft and exiting. *Ken Neubeck*

A Blue Angels aircraft is preparing for takeoff for a practice run, while maintenance personnel stay in formation and the head maintainer works with the pilot during preflight checks of flight control surfaces. *Ken Neubeck*

A Blue Angels aircraft is leaving as maintenance personnel stay in formation, while the head maintainer gives the go-ahead to the pilot. *Ken Neubeck*

Crew work on the nose landing gear of a Blue Angels aircraft. *Ken Neubeck*

The maintainer is working in the cockpit after the aircraft has arrived. Note that the pilot's helmet is on the nose landing-gear attachment. *Ken Neubeck*

An engine start has been performed on the #1 aircraft prior to takeoff for an airshow performance. *Ken Neubeck*

Maintenance personnel are doing some repairs on the wing area of the aircraft. *Ken Neubeck*

Maintenance personnel use portable equipment to fill the onboard liquid oxygen bottle, seen on the right. *Ken Neubeck*

On rare occasions, aircraft may have some equipment failures that would require leaving aircraft behind. This was the case with Blue Angels aircraft #5, which had some onboard oxygen issues that required the aircraft to be left behind after an airshow on Long Island, New York, in May 2016. This required a subsequent return visit of the "Fat Albert" C-130 aircraft to bring maintainers and repair equipment to correct the failure and allow the F/A-18 aircraft to go to the next destination. *Ken Neubeck*

Maintenance personnel are able to use the ramp of the C-130 to load the oxygen cart into the aircraft, under the watch of Capt. Kate Higgins, "Fat Albert" pilot. *Ken Neubeck*

Blue Angels #5 has just performed an engine start prior to leaving Long Island on June 21, 2016, after being laid up with maintenance issues for three weeks after the Memorial Day airshow.
Ken Neubeck

Blue Angels #5 returns to Pensacola on the same day that it left to rejoin the team, to the delight of the rest of the Blue Angels team. *US Navy photo by MCS 1st Class Andrea Perez*

On occasion, there may be issues with one of the starting six Blue Angels aircraft, and the maintenance crew members have to work to try to restore the aircraft to acceptable condition. Here the #1 aircraft is being worked on while the rest of the team is in the background, taking off for a practice run with some substitutions of number assignments. *Ken Neubeck*

It is not uncommon for aircraft numbers to be reassigned during the airshow. Sometimes the two-seater aircraft, which is normally the #7 media aircraft, is pressed into service with the team. Above is a substitution of the #5 into a #4 aircraft. The old decal is removed and a new decal is applied by maintenance personnel. *Ken Neubeck*

CHAPTER 10
Media Aircraft

TA-4J Blue Angels
media aircraft, circa
1980. *Mike Machat*

As the Blue Angels progressed during the 1950s, it was found that a special aircraft would be beneficial to perform several secondary tasks for the team, including flying members of the media. The team had media aircraft that accompanied the team for over five decades, as shown in the above chart.

Aircraft Type	Team Aircraft	Years Operated
TV-2	F9F	1952–1956
F9F-8T	F-11F	1957–1969
TA-4J	A-4F	1974–1986
F/A-18D	F/A-18C	1987 to present

The first such media aircraft was the TV-2, which rode with the team beginning in 1952. So not only was the aircraft a different model than the rest of the team, but it did not have the Blue Angels' blue-and-yellow paint scheme. Instead the aircraft was painted with checkerboard patterns on parts of the aircraft. The F9F-T model was one that was previously used by the Angels, serving the team until 1968. During the time that the team used the F-4J aircraft, there was an aircraft assigned to the team that was the same model, which made it easier since the F-4J was a two-seat aircraft to begin with. This trend of using the same model for the media aircraft as for the rest of the team continued when the team had the A-4 Skyhawks, with the two-seat trainer version of TA-4J being used up to the current time, whereas the team uses the two-seat version of the F/A-18.

The current Blue Angels team includes a two-seat F/A-18D Hornet that is assigned as #7, and it is used for a number of important tasks prior to and during each airshow event. This aircraft typically carries a backup Blue Angels pilot for the team and the public-relations officer. A few months before the airshow event, this aircraft will typically make a preliminary visit to the airport that will be used as the base for the team to take off and land during the airshow. This visit is made to inspect the airport, as well as to work with airport officers to go over all the logistics for the upcoming airshow and to work out any issues ahead of time.

The #7 aircraft is the first aircraft ro arrive during the week of the airshow event, usually the afternoon prior to the arral of the other six aircraft in the team. After this aircraft lands, it goes to the area of the runway where the temporary arresting-cable setup is installed, and it then conducts a simulated landing that catches the arresting cable. This cable functions as an emergency device should any issue aris during the landing of any of the blue Angels jets.

Throughout the following days of flying by the team, including during practice and the actual show, the #7 aircraft does not fly with the rest of the team. It is used primarily to conduct media flights, when a news reporter is riding in the back seat of the aircraft. Media personnel who request to go on this flight are medically screened some time prior to the event to ensure that the person can endure the requirements of flight, which include high g-force maneuvers. There may be five or six such flights that are conducted during the visit, depending on the weather and number of media people in queue.

The role of media aircraft became a major part of the team with the introduction of TV-2, BuNo 128676, in 1952. This aircraft would be assigned the number "0" on the tail. *Bill Larkins*

For many years the two F9F-8T aircraft flew with the team to conduct the media flights. Here is one of the aircraft at any one of the airshows in the 1960s. *Del Laughery*

There were two F9F-8T aircraft that were used as media aircraft beginning in 1957, during the time that the Blue Angels flew the F11F Tigers: BuNo 147404 (shown here), and BuNo 142470. Both aircraft would be assigned the number "7" on the tail. *Northrop Grumman History Center*

This is a TA-4J aircraft that was restored into the two-seat Blue Angels Number 7 aircraft by the Valiant Air Command Warbird Museum in Florida. This particular BuNo, 152867, did not actually serve with the Blue Angels team. *John Gourley*

Blue Angels F/A-18D two-seat aircraft at dawn on Long Island in 2016. The #7 aircraft precedes the rest of the team for an airshow event by one day, arriving the night before. *Ken Neubeck*

For airports not equipped with a permanent arresting-cable system, a temporary setup is used, such as this system installed at Republic Airport, New York, in 2012. *Ken Neubeck*

Blue Angels #7 has just caught the cable on this runway at Patrick AFB, Florida, in 2003. *John Gourley*

US Marine personnel extend the arresting cable assembly across the runway prior to Blue Angels #7 arriving. *Ken Neubeck*

This reporter is preparing for a media flight in the back-seat position of Blue Angels #7 on Long Island, New York, in May 2014. *Ken Neubeck*

The reporter is taking photos as the aircraft is preparing for takeoff from the runway. *Ken Neubeck*

To give the media flight some dramatic impact on takeoff, the pilot puts on the afterburners for full blast. *Ken Neubeck*

After a twenty-minute flight, which may include climbs and inversions, the pilot and reporter return back to the airport. *Ken Neubeck*

Lt. Tyler Davies performs one of the duties as the #7 pilot by providing the narration for the Blue Angels team during the Sioux Falls, South Dakota, airshow in July 2016. The following year, he would be moved to the #5 solo position for the team. *MCS 1st Class Andrea Perez*

Lt. Davies, in the #7 aircraft, has just completed the arresting-hook check on arrival at Republic Airport in May 2016, ahead of the team. The aircraft is waiting for personnel to remove the cable from the hook and put it back into the stowed position in the aircraft. *Ken Neubeck*

Blue Angels #7 is the most-photographed aircraft on the ground, since, in addition to the airshow, it makes the pre-airshow visit, as is the case in the left photograph, when the aircraft visited New York in November 2011 prior to the May 2012 airshow. The right photo is of the aircraft when it arrived ahead of the rest of the team in May 2018. *Ken Neubeck*

CHAPTER 11
Pilot Selection and Training

Blue Angels pilots are very experienced fliers. Many of the pilots have operational experience on carriers as well as trainer instructor experience. Up to the present time, there is a rigorous selection process for the individual pilots on the Blue Angels team and also for the pilots of the C-130 support aircraft. The process involves many highly qualified Navy and Marine Corps officers submitting applications to join the Blue Angels each year.

The current Blue Angels team and personnel select finalists to interview at the Blue Angels' home base at Naval Air Station Pensacola, Florida, during the week of the Pensacola Beach Air Show. The team makes selections at the conclusion of the interview week. Currently, pilots who are selected for the team have had significant experience flying the F/A-18 aircraft and other US Navy aircraft.

After selection, prospective team members join the team as "Khaki Newbies," referencing the uniform that they wear during the three-month learning period, which takes place at the Blue Angels' winter home in El Centro, California, beginning in early January.

The team practices at El Centro throughout January, February, and early March, flying several flights a day to perfect the demonstration. The ten-week, 120-flight time period will begin over the desert adjacent to El Centro, and once the team feels confident in the demonstration they will begin to fly over the airfield at El Centro. At the conclusion of this training period, the "Khaki Newbies" are then allowed to wear the trademark blue flight suit. At this time, there is also a transition process for the enlisted members of the team known as "cresting," when the new members "earn their crest."

The team has used El Centro as their winter training base for over fifty years. Southern California is the ideal place for the Blue Angels' winter training. By the beginning of April, the actual airshow season begins.

Service with the Blue Angels is typically for two years, and sometimes for three years if the pilot serves with the #7 media aircraft initially. After service, the pilot will return to active duty in the US Navy.

The 1958 Blue Angels team, led by their team leader, Ed Holley, (*third from the right*), with the members in front of the F11F Tiger. *Northrop Grumman History Center*

Blue Angels #1 through #6 have just arrived at Republic Airport, New York, in preparation for the Jones Beach Air Show in 2014. Pilots are preparing to depart from their aircraft. *Ken Neubeck*

Pilots from Blue Angels #1 through #6 are meeting up with the pilots from Blue Angels #7 shortly after arrival on Long Island, New York. They will be conducting media interviews next to their aircraft. *Ken Neubeck*

Blue Angels pilots salute while walking in formation at their winter training facility at El Centro, California, in March 2018. All formations are practiced. *US Navy photo by Petty Officer 2nd Class Jess Gray*

Blue Angels pilots from four aircraft walk in formation approaching the pilot from aircraft #2, where they will march to join up with the pilot from the last aircraft. *Ken Neubeck*

Lt. Cdr. Nate Barton was a member of the 2014 Blue Angels team and is seen here, shortly after arrival, being interviewed by the media next to his #3 F/A-18C aircraft at Republic Airport, Farmingdale, New York. Each team member is assigned a number of media people during the pilot interview session. *Ken Neubeck*

Lt. Cdr. Barton is the pilot in the #3 aircraft during a landing upon return to Republic Airport after performing at Jones Beach, New York, in May 2014. *Ken Neubeck*

Lt. Kevin Davis is greeting his back-seat rider in the #7 media aircraft in October 2006. The next year, Davis would be flying the #6 opposing solo aircraft. *US Navy photo by CMCS Monica Hallman*

Lt. Davis lost his life during an airshow performance on April 21, 2007. His flag-draped coffin is taken from the "Fat Albert" C-130 at Pensacola on April 25, in the presence of the entire Blue Angels team during the funeral procession. *US Navy photo by MCS 2nd Class Ryan Courtade*

Marine captain Jeff Kuss is signing autographs with the crowds during an airshow event in March 2016. Public relations is a major part of being a Blue Angel. *US Navy photo by MCS 2nd Class Daniel M. Young*

Capt. Kuss is flying aircraft #6 during practice on Long Island on May 27, 2016. The next week, he would perish in a crash when executing a low-transition/split-S maneuver during practice in Smyrna, Tennessee. *Ken Neubeck*

The loss of a Blue Angels pilot due to tragedy is felt not only by the team but also by the communities who have watched the team perform. The #5 aircraft was left behind due to mechanical problems during the 2016 Memorial Day weekend airshow on Long Island. The next show, in Smyrna, Tennessee, was when Capt. Kuss lost his life. When the "Fat Albert" C-130 and the team returned to fix the aircraft, there was a spontaneous outpouring of support, with sympathy flags being placed on the fence of Republic Airport for Capt. Kuss and the Blue Angels team. *Ken Neubeck*

Upon returning either from a practice run or actual airshow performance, the team will walk in formation past each aircraft, as seen in the top photo, then greet each other, as in the bottom-left photo. After that, the team will gather near a support area to undergo a debriefing, where aircraft issues of concern are discussed with the maintenance personnel for the team, as seen in the photo on the bottom right. *Ken Neubeck*

Quite often during the week when the Angels are based at a location for an airshow, members of the team will mingle with the crowds. Here, Capt. Tyler Davis from the #5 aircraft is engaging with spectators at Republic Airport when the Angels visited Long Island in May 2018. *Ken Neubeck*

Capt. Katie Higgins, "Fat Albert" pilot, greets onlookers at the fence during a special repair mission of disabled Blue Angels aircraft at Republic Airport, Long Island, in June 2016. The Angels make every attempt to meet with the general public during any visit. *Ken Neubeck*

CHAPTER 12
Airshow Maneuvers

The Blue Angels will not fly when there is significant rain or poor visibility, as was the case on May 27, 2018, for the Jones Beach Air Show in New York. *Ken Neubeck*

The Blue Angels average about sixty shows a year at thirty different locations. Thus, there is a need to have the same well-defined set of routines and maneuvers in order to maintain consistency and, most of all, safety. The Blue Angels refine these routines during the off-season at El Centro, where the team practices six days a week and accumulates a total of 120 training missions.

There are three different sets of routines—the High show, the Low show, and the Flat show. The selection of which show will be performed on the day of the airshow will depend on a number of factors, such as the weather, the cloud ceiling, and the prevailing wind. The following table shows the setup for these shows:

Name	Ceiling	Maneuvers Available
High Show	10,000 feet	34
Low Show	4,500 feet	30
Flat Show	1,000 feet	29

As has been established over the years with previous Blue Angels teams, there are specific job titles for each of the different members/ aircraft of the Blue Angels team:

#1 Team Leader (Boss)

#2 Right Wing

#3 Left Wing

#4 Slot

#5 Lead Solo

#6 Opposing Solo

#7 Influencer Pilot and Narrator

#8 Transport ("Fat Albert")

Blue Angels 1 through 4 will perform the delta formation, with the two solos aircraft, 5 and 6, performing around them for certain maneuvers as well as individual maneuvers away from the team. All six aircraft do perform together in the delta-style maneuvers.

The following pages show some of the maneuvers in pictorial form, along with photos as to how the maneuvers are performed during the show. Most team maneuvers come out initially either from the diamond or the delta formation. Some maneuvers such as the Fortus are used in all three types of shows and are indicated as such in the diagrams. The maneuver descriptions come from the *Blue Angels Maneuvers Manual*.

Getting a basic understanding and being able to identify these maneuvers add to the enjoyment of watching the show, as does taking photos.

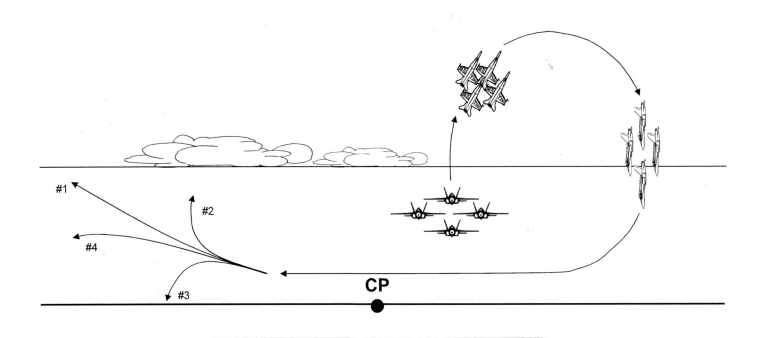

SPECTATOR AREA

Barrel Roll Break

Maneuver: Ingressing from in front at 2,000 feet, crowd right, the diamond formation will commence a vertical climb. Approaching 1.7 nautical miles (NM) from critical point (CP), they will roll the formation 90 degrees to the left and complete the backside of the looping maneuver. As the formation passes through the horizon at approximately 500 feet AGL, they will split into three separate directions: #1 and #4 will exit out of the show line, while #2 and #3 will egress 90 degrees in front of and behind the crowd, respectively. The rendezvous will be conducted behind the crowd. **Used in High show only.**

Blue Angels F/A-18 #1 through #4 perform the last portion of the barrel roll break at Seattle, Washington, in July 2015. *US Navy photo by MSC 2nd Andrea Perez*

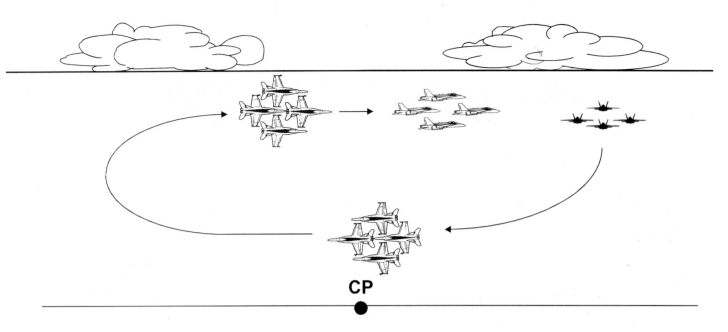

CP

SPECTATOR AREA

Burner 270

Maneuver: Ingressing from crowd right in front of the crowd, the formation approaches in diamond formation. Approaching CP, they commence a right turn, selecting afterburner as they execute a 270-degree turn in front of the crowd and egress to crowd right behind the crowd. **Used in Flat show only.**

Blue Angels F/A-18s #1 through #4 are seen here during execution of the Burner 270 maneuver in Michigan in June 2018. *US Navy photo by MCS 2nd Class Timothy Schumaker*

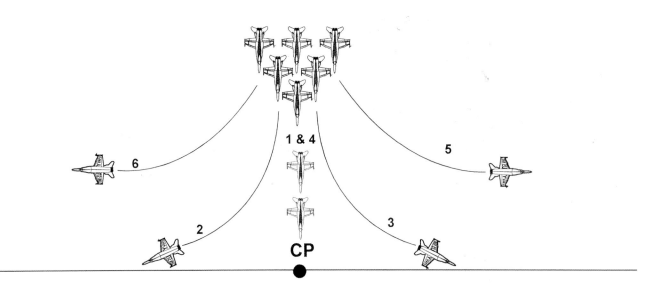

1 & 4

6

5

2

3

CP

SPECTATOR AREA

Delta Breakout

Maneuver: The delta will roll out in a head-on setup and commence a climb. One nautical mile in front of the crowd, #1 jet will call "Ready, break!" and the delta will split. Aircraft #1 will pull up into a steady 2 g climb straight ahead; #5 and #6 will pull outboard in a steady 2 g 60-degree angle of bank; #2 and #3 will pull outboard in a steady 2 g, 45 degree angle of bank, and offset by 45 degrees. #1 and #4 will continue straight ahead and exit behind the crowd, rendezvousing with the other four aircraft. **Used in High, Low, and Flat shows.**

The Blue Angels perform a delta breakout directly over Alcatraz in October 2016. The Angels are regular visitors to San Francisco, where they perform over the Bay area. *US Navy photo by MCS 3rd Class Dominick Cremeans*

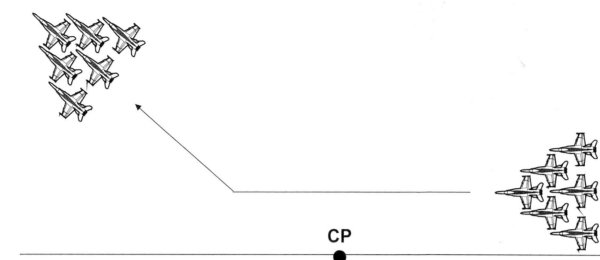

CP

SPECTATOR AREA

Delta Flat Pass

Maneuver: Ingressing straight and level at 200 feet AGL from crowd right, all six aircraft will perform a flat pass on the 500-foot show line and exit in front of the crowd to set up for the delta breakout or head-on. **Used in High, Low, and Flat shows.**

The Blue Angels F/A-18 team is seen here flying in classic delta flat-pass formation going over Republic Airport in Farmingdale, New York, in May 2018. From this formation, the team performs a breakout that results in each aircraft landing individually.
Ken Neubeck

CP

SPECTATOR AREA

Diamond 360

Maneuver: While remaining in the diamond formation, the four aicraft executes a nonaerobatic right to left circular pass at less than a 60-degree angle of bank (AOB), crossing over CP at a minimum altitude of 200 feet. **Used in the High, Low, and Flat shows.**

The Blue Angels perform a diamond 360 maneuver, in which they fly in tight, four-ship diamond formation over Ocean City, Maryland, in June 2015. *US Navy photo by MCS 2nd Class Andrea Perez*

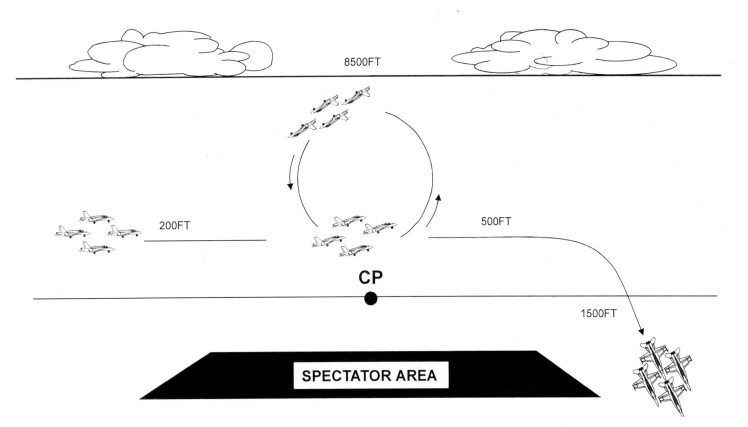

8500FT

200FT

500FT

1500FT

CP

SPECTATOR AREA

Diamond Dirty Loop

Maneuver: In the diamond formation, all four aircraft will complete a loop over CP on the show line, with the landing gear and hooks extended. **Used in High show.**

The Blue Angels perform the inverted portion of the diamond dirty loop in Sioux Falls, South Dakota, in July 2016. *US Navy photo by MCS 1st Class Daniel M. Young*

CP

SPECTATOR AREA

Diamond Flat Pass

Maneuver: The diamond will perform a flat pass at 200 feet AGL on the 500-foot show line from crowd right to crowd left. **Used in Low show.**

Blue Angels F/A-18s #1 through #4 are seen here in the classic diamond flat-pass formation going over Republic Airport in Farmingdale, New York. The #1 aircraft is in the lead position, #2 and #3 are the wings, and #4 is in the rear, or slot, position.
Ken Neubeck

DIRTY ROLL

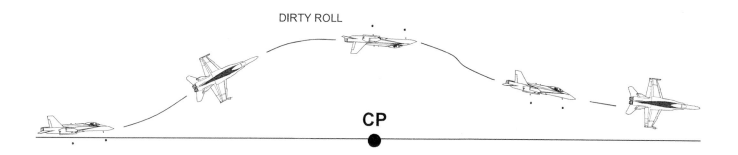

CP

SPECTATOR AREA

Dirty Roll on Takeoff: #5

Maneuver: A left or right 360-degree roll away from the crowd while raising the landing gear. If this maneuver cannot be performed in the aerobatic box between 1,200 and 1,500 feet, it must be executed in the aerobatic box beyond the crowd line. It can be flown from either direction, on the basis of CP and prevailing wind. The show line clear is a climbing turn behind the crowd. **Used in High show and Low show.**

Lt. Ryan Chamberlain begins to perform a dirty roll on takeoff in his #5 aircraft at the airshow in St. Louis, Missouri, in May 2016. *US Navy photo by MSC 1st Class Andrea Perez*

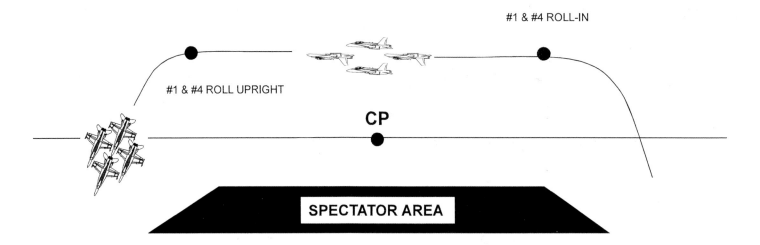

#1 & #4 ROLL-IN

#1 & #4 ROLL UPRIGHT

CP

SPECTATOR AREA

Double Farvel

Maneuver: Aircraft #1 and #4 roll inverted simultaneously at 1 NM while #2 and #3 remain upright. Maintaining a diamond formation, they commence a flat pass at 200 feet. No later than 1 NM past CP, #1 and #4 sequentially roll upright in a climb. **Used in High, Low, and Flat shows.**

Blue Angels F/A-18 #1 and #4 fly inverted during this maneuver, while #2 and #3 stay upright during the execution of the double-farvel maneuver conducted at Barksdale AFB, Louisiana, in May 2017. *US Navy photo by MSC 2nd Class Ian Cotter*

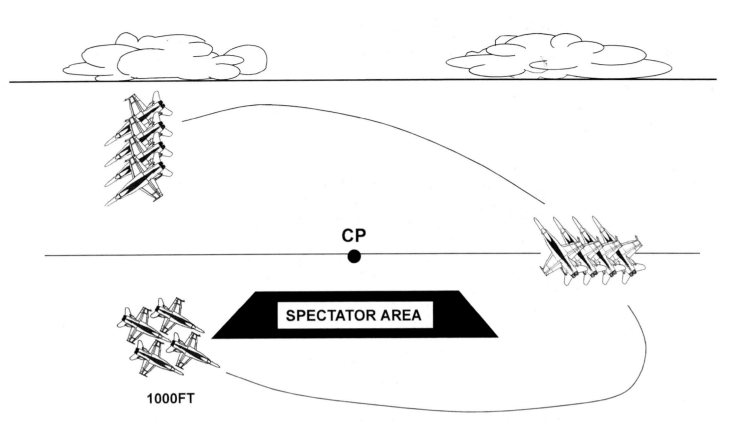

CP

SPECTATOR AREA

1000FT

Echelon Parade

Maneuver: In right echelon, the diamond executes a right-to-left nonaerobatic circular pass at approximately 60-degree AOB, crossing over CP at a minimum altitude of 200 feet. **Used in High, Low, and Flat shows.**

Blue Angels F/A-18s #1 through #4 perform one of the standard maneuvers during the airshow: the echelon parade, where the aircraft line up in a slightly staggered formation as they fly over the crowd. *US Navy photo by MSC 2nd Class Ian Cotter*

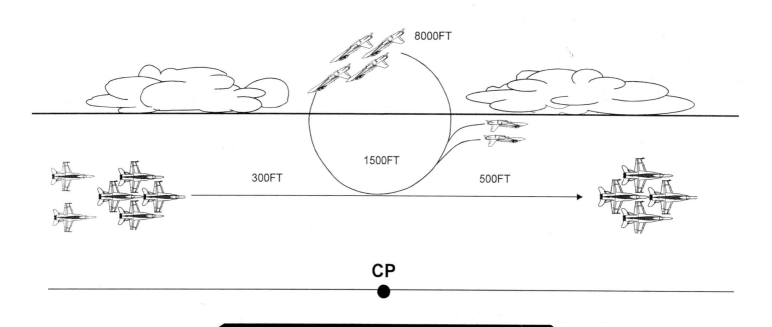

8000FT

1500FT

300FT 500FT

CP

SPECTATOR AREA

Fleur-de-Lis

Maneuver: Approaching the show line in a double "V" formation, the six aircraft will commence a climb. At approximately 2,000 feet prior to CP, all six aircraft will split simultaneously. The two solos will execute 1½ rolls and exit crowd right initially, then turn behind the crowd. The four diamond aircraft will rendezvous during their looping maneuver over CP and egress in diamond crowd right to crowd right in front of the crowd. **Used in High show.**

Blue Angels F/A-18s #1 through #4 go in one direction, whereas #5 and #6 peel off to go in another direction in Cleveland, Ohio, in 2016. Aircraft #1 through #4 form the diamond, while #5 and #6 ride on the outside of the rear row. *US Navy photo by MCS 1st Class Andrea Perez*

5 ROLLS UPRIGHT

5 ROLLS INVERTED

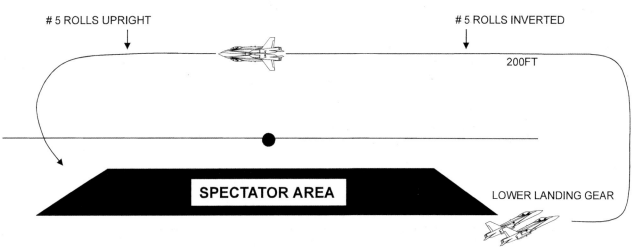

200FT

SPECTATOR AREA

LOWER LANDING GEAR

Fortus

Maneuver: Both #5 and #6 aircraft will approach from crowd right in the dirty configuration; #5 will roll inverted at the edge of the aerobatic box at a minimum of 200 feet, while #6 will move to an abeam position upright, creating a mirror-image effect. At CP, both aircraft will climb. At ¾ NM, #5 will roll upright and both aircraft will clear crowd left behind the crowd. **Used in High, Low, and Flat shows.**

Blue Angels #5 flies inverted and #6 flies upright in performing the Fortus maneuver over Virginia Beach in September 2017, creating a mirror-image effect to the crowd. *US Navy photo by MSC 1st Class Daniel M. Young*

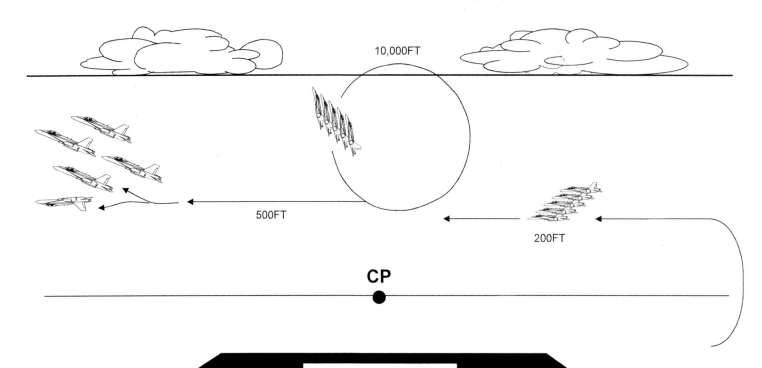

10,000FT

500FT

200FT

CP

SPECTATOR AREA

Line Abreast Loop

Maneuver: At approximately 3½ NM, aircraft #1, #2, #3, #4, and #5 transition to a line abreast formation. Approaching CP, they complete a loop. Egressing crowd left, aircraft #1 through #4 shift back to diamond and detach from #5. **Used in High, Low, and Flat shows.**

The Blue Angels form a line abreast maneuver over Cherry Point, North Carolina, in May 2018, with aircraft #1 through #5. *US Navy photo by MCS 1std Class Daniel M. Young*

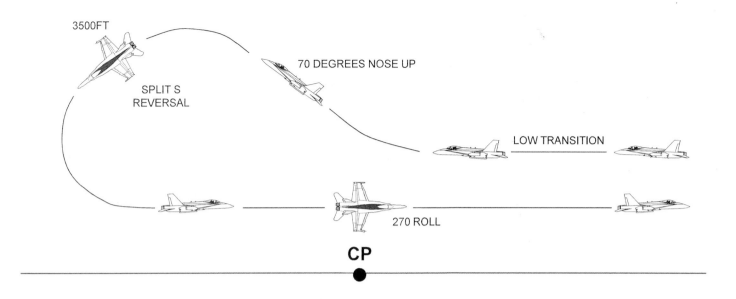

3500FT

SPLIT S
REVERSAL

70 DEGREES NOSE UP

LOW TRANSITION

270 ROLL

CP

SPECTATOR AREA

Low Transition / Split-S on Takeoff: #6

Maneuver: Aircraft #6 will execute a low transition, and at 285 KCAS (calibrated airspeed in knots) he will pull to 70 degrees nose up. At a minimum of 3,500 feet, he will roll the aircraft 180 degrees and complete a split-S reversal. Passing CP, he will roll the aircraft 270 degrees and clear behind the crowd. **Used in High show and Low show.**

Capt. Jeff Kuss in his #6 aircraft performs the low-altitude portion of the low-transition/split-S maneuver on takeoff at the St. Louis airshow in May 2016. *US Navy photo by MSC 1st Class Andrea Perez*

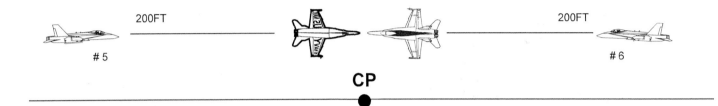

200FT   **200FT**

5   CP   # 6

SPECTATOR AREA

Opposing Knife Edge

Maneuver: At CP, each pilot will roll his aircraft into a 90-degree angle of bank prior to the cross. After the cross, both aircraft will roll upright and clear in front of the crowd. **Used in High, Low, and Flat shows.**

The two opposing solos (#5 and #6) pass each other in the opposing knife edge maneuver over Virginia Beach in September 2017. *US Navy photo by MSC 1st Class Daniel M. Young*

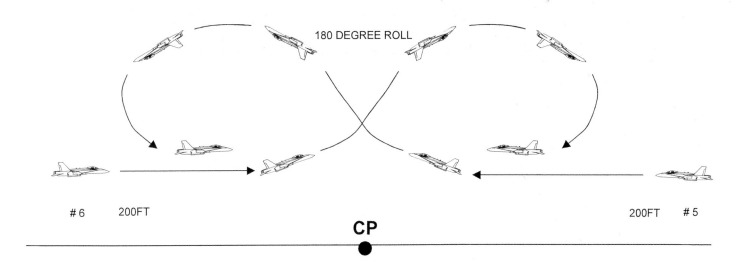

180 DEGREE ROLL

6   200FT

200FT   # 5

CP

SPECTATOR AREA

Vertical Pitch

Maneuver: Approaching CP at a minimum of 50 feet, each aircraft pulls 65–70 degrees nose up and then rolls 180 degrees. Both aircraft complete a split-S and cross over CP. At CP, each pilot performs a right 360-degree roll, then clears behind the crowd. **Used in High show.**

The two opposing solos (#5 and #6) pass each other in the vertical pitch maneuver in Michigan in September 2017. *US Navy photo by MSC 1st Class Daniel M. Young*

Blue Angels A-4 aircraft #1 through #6 are flying in formation in 1984, with #1 aircraft on top of the formation. The photo has been taken from the rear of a KC-10 tanker during aerial refueling and the team is in a compressed delta formation where all six aircraft can be seen. *US Navy photo by PH2 Paul O' Mara*

Blue Angels F/A-18 aircraft #1 through #6 are flying in formation in 2016, in a photo taken over thirty-two years after the top one. Similar to the top photo, this photo was taken in the same manner, from the back of the tanker, and the team is flying in a compressed delta formation. The aircraft may change but the maneuvers remain consistently the same between teams over the years. *US Navy photo by MCS 2nd Class Daniel M. Young*

This is an underside view of the delta formation performed by F11F Blue Angels jets in the 1960s.
US Navy

Blue Angels A-4 aircraft are landing in a diamond formation at the Naval Air Station (NAS) in Pensacola, Florida in May of 1969.
US Navy photo by Paul O' Mara PH2

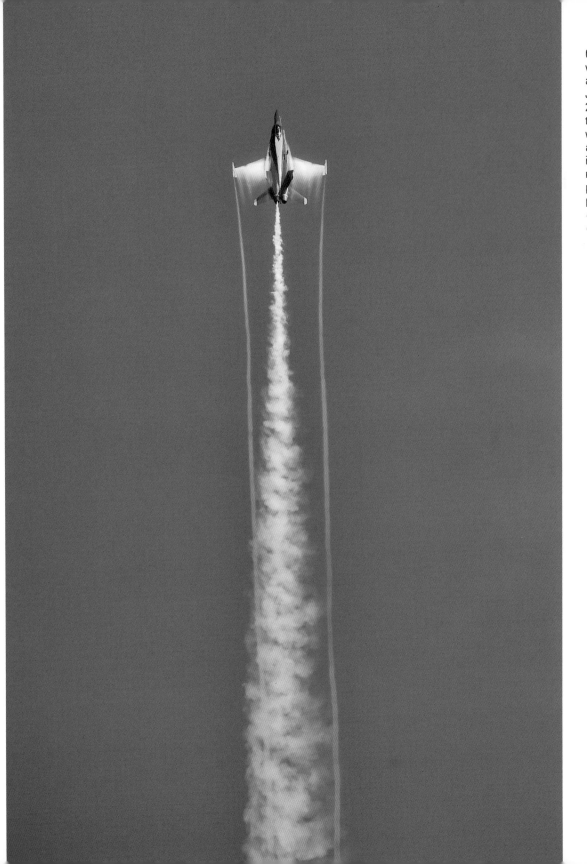

Cmdr. Frank Weisser is performing vertical-roll maneuvers in his #6 aircraft at an airshow in Jacksonville, Florida, in November 2016. The water vapor pulling off the aircraft fuselage, combined with the contrails off the wing tips and the smoke, makes for a very impressive display during this maneuver. Keep in mind that the pilots do not wear a G suit when pulling these high-g maneuvers. *US Navy photo by Petty Officer 1st Class Daniel M, Young*

A close-up view of the vertical-roll maneuver shows Lt. Craig Olsonk in the #6 aircraft performing this maneuver during an airshow in Pensacola, Florida, in July 2004. As the pilot goes vertical approaching supersonic speed, water vapor condensation or vapor fog is coming off the wings due to sudden pressure drop over the wings during the steep aircraft climb. *US Navy photo by Photographer's Mate 2nd Class Ryan Courtade*

The Blue Angels are in the process of performing a vertical-break maneuver during the airshow in Los Angeles, California, in March 2016, shortly after their winter training at El Centro. *US Navy photo by MSC 2nd Class Daniel M. Young*

Lt. Ryan Chamberlain performs the solo minimum-radius turn in his #5 aircraft, at the Jacksonville, Florida, airshow in November 2016. *US Navy photo by MSC 1st Class Daniel M. Young*

A Blue Angels aircraft is in inverted flight during execution of the double-farvel maneuver during a practice run over Pensacola Beach, Florida, in July 2011. *US Navy photo by MSC 3rd Class Andrew Johnson*

These two photos were taken a day apart but show the same event of the team in action from two different perspectives. The first photo is taken of the team in the delta formation, passing over an industrial area from the south near Republic Airport on Long Island, shortly after the team has released smoke from its tanks. The second photo is a view from Republic Airport of the team in the distance, coming from the south at the moment of the smoke release, giving the appearance of an explosion in the sky. These photos show the remarkable consistency of the team, which is the result of many hours of training.
Ken Neubeck

CHAPTER 13
Museum Displays

There are two Blue Angels cockpit trainers in the National Naval Aviation Museum in Pensacola: one for the F-4, and one for the F11F shown below. *Ken Neubeck*

This Blue Angels F11F display aircraft, BuNo 141832, hangs from the ceiling at the entrance to the Cradle of Aviation Museum in Garden City, Long Island, New York. This aircraft did do service with the Angels during the time period from 1959 to 1968. The aircraft has been restored to show the markings of the #5 aircraft that was flown by Lt. Norman Gandia, a Long Islander, who flew with the Angels from 1966 to 1967. *Ken Neubeck*

In addition to viewing the Blue Angels during an airshow, there are many aircraft on display throughout the US in museums and as airport gate guards that are accessible to the public. Some of these aircraft were the actual aircraft that were used by the Blue Angels, while some others are retired US Navy aircraft that were painted into Blue Angels colors but did not serve on the team. Examples of a few of these displays are shown here.

This Blue Angels F11F display aircraft, BuNo 141796, has just been repainted to resume its role as a gate guard to Walker field at Grand Junction Airport, Colorado. The volunteers are using a lift to put the aircraft back on two posts. *Ben Peck*

This Blue Angels F11F display is in its final position near the mountains of Colorado. This aircraft, BuNo 141796, did actual service with the Blue Angels, beginning in 1959, and is on loan from the National Naval Aviation Museum. The current Blue Angels team has made airshow appearances at this airport. *Ben Peck*

This Blue Angels F11F display is in the Pima Air & Science Museum in Tucson, Arizona. This particular aircraft, BuNo 141824, did service with the Angels and flew again in 1974 as part of the thrust-reverser evaluation program, after which it was restored into Blue Angels colors. *Ken Neubeck*

A major display of the Blue Angels A-4 aircraft is the simulated diamond formation of #1 through #4, hanging from the ceiling in the National Naval Aviation Museum in Pensacola, Florida. *John Gourley*

This Blue Angels A-4F display is on Interstate 10 near Milton, Florida. This A-4F, BuNo 148490, did not actually serve with the Angels, but it was restored to the colors of the team. *John Gourley*

A Blue Angels A-4F display aircraft, BuNo 148490, is mounted on a pole on Interstate 10, outside the US Navy facility in Pensacola, Florida. *John Gourley*

The USS *Intrepid* Sea, Air, and Space Museum in New York City features a number of US Navy aircraft, including this restored Blue Angels F11F display located on the flight deck in the general public viewing area. *Ken Neubeck*

The Blue Angels F11F display aircraft, BuNo 141884, on the USS *Intrepid* was flown by Lew Chatham as the #5 solo position for three years with the team, from 1961 through 1963. Chatham would eventually reach the rank of rear admiral. *Ken Neubeck*

Two F9F-8T aircraft were used during the history of the team: BuNo 147404 and BuNo 142470. The restored aircraft shown here on display at a public park in Woodbridge, New York, which did not serve with the Angels, is another F9F-8T aircraft but was restored and painted in the Blue Angels scheme. *Ken Neubeck*

This is another F9F-8T display aircraft, BuNo 146417, that has been restored but was not originally a Blue Angels aircraft. This aircraft is on display at the Evergreen Museum in Washington. *Ben Peck*

CHAPTER 14
The Future:
F/A-18E/F Super Hornet

By 2018, the US Navy began the process of rotating older F/A-18 Super Hornet where the older F/A-18C and F/A-18D Hornets out of the fleet and replacing them with them with F/A-18E and F/A-18F Super Hornets. The plan was for the Blue Angels to also receive the Super Hornet F/A-18E for the six aircraft team, with the two-seat F/A-18F Super Hornet designated for the # 7 Blue Angels media aircraft. As the original F/A-18C and D model was getting older and harder to support in terms of parts, this was a logical move.

The Super Hornet is a heavier and larger aircraft than the original Hornet aircraft, with similar performance characteristics. It is active in the US Navy carrier fleet and has been used in combat action in recent years in different theaters of war. The Blue Angels began using the Super Hornet model in the 2021 show season and this continues to the present time.

Regardless of the aircraft that may be used in the future for the team, the mission of the Blue Angels remains the same: showcasing the pride and professionalism of the United States Navy and Marine Corps by inspiring a culture of excellence and service to country through flight demonstrations and community outreach.

An F/A-18F Super Hornet is shown arriving at Republic Airport, Long Island, in May 2012, for participation in the annual Jones Beach Air Show. *Ken Neubeck*

Captain Eric Doyle has just delivered the first Blue Angels Super Hornet aircraft to the Blue Angels team at Naval Air Station, Pensacola, on a rainy day on July 27, 2002. *US Navy photo by MSC2nd Class Cody Hendrix*

Captain Eric Doyle is speaking with Blue Angels team leader Cmdr. Brian Kesselring during the transfer in July of 2020, which was during the COVID19 pandemic and both men are wearing mask protection. *US Navy photo by MSC2nd Class Cody Hendrix*

Blue Angels Super Hornet F/A-18E single seat aircraft is seen here at Long Island Republic Airport during the Memorial Day weekend of 2022 on its way during a practice run during the Jones Beach Airshow. This was the team's first return to Long Island since 2018 as the 2020 event was cancelled due to the COVID19 pandemic. *Ken Neubeck*

Super Hornet F/A-18F two-seat aircraft is being prepped during a media flight conducted during Memorial Day weekend of 2022 at Republic Airport in Long Island. The two engine intakes for the Super Hornet are rectangular in lieu of the oval shape of the older Hornet models used by the team. *Ken Neubeck*

Heritage flight consists of F/A-18 Blue Angels #1 flying with an F6F Hellcat and F8F Bearcat in March 2017 over the Salton Sea, California. The vintage aircraft were the original aircraft models that the Blue Angels flew in 1946. *US Navy photo by Petty Officer 2nd Class Ian Cotter*

A Blue Angels team flying in mass takeoff, with contrails streaming off the wings. The takeoff consists of #1 through #4, followed by #5 and #6, leaving Long Island in May 2018 to go to the next airshow in Pax River, Maryland. The #7 aircraft left the day before to conduct their pre-airshow activities. *Ken Neubeck*

This is a painting that shows the progression of aircraft during the seventy-year history of the Blue Angels, beginning with the F6F Hellcat (*top*) down to the F/A-18 (*bottom*). *US Navy*